THE ART OF MORALITY

UNDERSTANDING MORAL VALUES

Isaiah Netsianda

eBook ISBN: 978-0-6397-8893-7
Paperback ISBN: 978-0-6397-8892-0

Contact Details of the Publisher
Phone: +27 87 061 2192
Email: info@netsiandabooks.com
Website: www.netsiandabooks.com

Ordering information

Ordering in bulk for schools, libraries and organizations is
available at discounted rates. For such orders send an email
to orders@netsiandabooks.com

TABLE OF CONTENTS

PREFACE

The journey towards enlightenment is one that lies at the core of our existence. Throughout history, people have always had questions about what it means to be a good person. In this book, "The Art Of Morality: Understanding Moral Values," I attempt to explain moral values, explore the profound impact of moral values on our lives and share a few morals that I reckon are essential to have.

This book doesn't claim to be the sole truth about morality, it is the product of my own personal experiences and an exploration of the depths of human morality and the remarkable power it holds. As a person who advocates for ethical living, I have devoted myself to studying, reflecting and engaging in conversations about the nature of morality. I believe that moral values shape both our own lives and the collective destiny of humanity. Through this book, I also aim to share the knowledge I have about morals. I believe that by understanding and embracing moral values, we can create a better world.

Firstly, I will explore the meaning and the general impact of morals in our lives. In a society that often prioritizes personal gain, we witness dishonesty, cruelty and disregard for others becoming prevalent. Whilst in a society that promotes togetherness and compassion, we witness honesty, kindness and a regard for others. By discussing what morals are and making people aware of the impact of morals, I hope to underscore the urgency of reclaiming our moral compass.

Secondly, I will share eleven moral values that foster healthy and ethical living. Honesty, compassion, sharing, respect, discipline, fairness, courage, humility, optimism, forgiveness and gratitude are among the values shared in this section. Drawing my personal experiences and real life observations, I explore the benefits of embodying these values, both for ourselves and our society. I invite readers to reflect on the ways in which moral values can elevate our relationships, decision-making processes and overall well-being.

Lastly, but not least I will offer guidance on how to develop and nurture moral values. Recognizing that personal growth is an ongoing process, I provide readers with concrete strategies and exercises to integrate these values into their lives.

It is essential to acknowledge that morality is not a fixed set of rules. Instead, it is an evolving concept. While I offer insights and suggestions, I encourage readers to engage critically, challenge assumptions and form their own conclusions. Morality is personal and subjective and we can only enrich our understanding by exploring different perspectives. I am aware of the challenges and complexities that arise when navigating moral problems. The world we inhabit is rife with moral ambiguity. However, by equipping ourselves with a strong moral foundation, we can navigate these challenges better.

"The Art Of Morality: Understanding Moral Values" is an invitation to embark on a journey of understanding moral values. It is urging us to reassess our values, make conscious choices and actively contribute to a better world.

As we embark on the exploration of moral values, let us approach it with an open mind. Let us recognize that our actions, no matter how small, have the power to ripple out and shape the world around us. Together, we can create a future where morality is a lived experience.

I invite you, the reader, to explore the pages in this book and hope that the contents of this book illuminate your path, inspire your actions and moral consciousness.

Understanding Moral Values

In this chapter I will discuss what moral values are and explain a few types of morals. Also, I will talk about both the impacts of lacking moral values and having good moral values with hopes of helping you grow your knowledge about moral values and their influence on how we behave and who we are.

What are morals? Morals are a set of beliefs that help people distinguish between right and wrong, good and bad or ethical and unethical. They help us make decisions, shape our behavior and influence how people interact with others. Morals often stem from cultural norms, religious teachings and personal experiences. Moral values can be personal, cultural, religious, universal and professional. Each type of morals emphasize different aspects of ethical conduct.

Religious morals are based on the teachings and doctrines of a particular religion. They provide guidance on conduct and ethical behavior, often grounded on spiritual teachings of faith. Compassion, justice, forgiveness and love for others are among the values commonly found in the teachings of faith. Meanwhile, universal morals, as the term suggests, are values that are considered as universally applicable across different societies. They are shared values that transcend cultural and religious differences and are often agreed to be ethical and significant to humanity. They help us coexist with each other. Examples of universal morals include honesty, fairness and respect for others.

Professional morals on the other hand, are standards and conduct specific to a particular field of work. They outline the responsibilities and guidelines that professionals should adhere to. Professional morals differ with disciplines and industries. To mention a few, professional morals often include integrity, confidentiality and accountability.

Meanwhile, personal morals refer to a person's beliefs about right and wrong. They are influenced by personal experiences, introspection and self-reflection. Personal morals shape a person's character, behavior and influence their daily choices. While, cultural morals are formed from norms and customs of a particular culture. These reflect the understanding of what is considered acceptable or unacceptable in a certain culture. Cultural morals play a significant role in shaping our behavior, relationships and what is expected of us by society.

Morals evolve and are different between people and societies. Understanding morals can provide insights on ethical values that guide human behavior and shape societies.

In a society that lacks moral values, we witness negative consequences that permeate different aspects of our lives. When people prioritize personal gain, we see societies deteriorating. An apparent impact of lacking morals is the proliferation of dishonesty. When personal gain is a driving force, people lie, cheat and engage in deceitful practices to achieve their personal goals. Dishonesty does not only undermine trust between people but also erodes integrity in the society. Without strong morals, people engage in unethical behaviors and undermine trust - a necessity for meaningful cohesion. Moreover, the lack of moral values results in cruelty. In a society that lacks morals, people disregard the well-being of others. When people live without considering others, their actions often cause harm. This can often be seen in forms such as exploitation, manipulation and sometimes even as violence. The lack of empathy and compassion results in people being disconnected from each other, disregarding the needs and struggles of others. Also, lacking moral values can contribute to the erosion of societal standards. Without a shared understanding of right and wrong, people engage in behaviors that go against justice, fairness and equality. This leads to injustices and discrimination. In the absence of moral guidance, societies find it difficult to establish and maintain social order, resulting in divisions.

Lacking moral values also has a huge effect on institutions and governance. When moral values are disregarded, corruption and unethical practices are common. Without strong morals, people in power prioritize themselves, leading to a misuse of resources, abuse of power and a lack of accountability. This undermines public trust in institutions and erodes a functioning democracy. The lack of moral values has detrimental effects on the overall well-being and happiness of people. When personal gain is prioritized at the expense of moral values such as kindness, empathy and compassion, people feel empty and experience a sense of dissatisfaction and disconnection. True connections and meaningful relationships are built on shared values and lacking these values lead to alienation and sometimes a lack of purpose.

In a society that embraces good morals, we witness positive impacts that shape the well-being of people and foster a healthy and thriving community. When people prioritize ethical considerations and have values such as honesty, kindness and regard for others, we witness a happy and a more content community.

The fundamental impacts of having good morals are trust and integrity. When people act with honesty and transparency, they build a foundation of trust in their interactions with others. Trust forms the basis of good relationships, collaboration and a sense of security in the community. In a society where good morals prevail, people can rely on one another, fostering unity, social cohesion and collective progress. Kindness is an essential aspect of good morals. It has an impact on people and society as a whole. Acts of kindness, whether small or huge, have the power to uplift people and can strengthen bonds between people. Practicing acts of kindness leads to an improved well-being, empathetic and a supportive environment where people feel valued and cared for. Furthermore, having good morals fosters responsibility and accountability. When people embrace moral values, they understand the impact of their actions on others. This encourages responsible behavior and ethical decision-making.

People who have the willingness to take ownership of their own actions help build a society where people are held accountable for their actions, a society where people think about the consequences of their choices. Good morals contribute to the development of a united community with social interconnectedness. When people prioritize the well-being of others and have a regard for others, a supportive and inclusive society is often created as a result. Good moral values play a significant role in shaping ethical leadership and governance. When people with strong moral values gain power, they often prioritize the common good. They make fair decisions and act in the best interest of the community. Leaders with good morals inspire trust and transparency. They set an example for others and promote integrity and responsible governance.

Lastly but not least, the impact of good moral values inspire well-being and happiness. When people align their actions with moral values, they experience fulfillment, find purpose and inner harmony. Living life with good moral values improves self-esteem and contributes to one's mental and emotional well-being. People who embody morals often find themselves experiencing contentment in their lives.

Now that I discussed what moral values are, shared and explained the types of moral values, I hope you have an idea or a clear understanding and have grown your knowledge about morals. In the next chapters I will share some of the values I believe good and effective people have. These values help build better, healthy, inclusive and supportive communities.

HONESTY FOSTERS TRUST AND INTEGRITY

One of the most vital values that a good person has is honesty. Honesty encompasses truthfulness and transparency in one's words and actions. It is a fundamental value that guides us to represent reality accurately. It also helps refrain from deception or falsehoods. The practice of honesty shapes our character and has a profound impact on different aspects of our lives and in the society. Honesty creates a foundation of trust and integrity in relationships. When we consistently act honestly, we create an atmosphere where open and authentic communication can thrive. Honest people can be reliable, as they are known to provide accurate information and can fulfill commitments. They act with integrity. Trust is crucial in relationships of all sorts, as it fosters a sense of security and mutual respect.

Moreover, honesty promotes effective problem-solving. When people engage in honest communications, they openly express their thoughts, concerns and views, creating a conducive atmosphere to foster productive dialogue. Honest conversations enable understanding of different viewpoints. They facilitate the search for solutions that are beneficial to everyone. This promotes collaboration, leading to better outcomes in relationships, workplaces and communities. Honesty also plays a vital role in personal growth. Being honest with yourself involves acknowledging one's strengths, weaknesses and leaves a room for improvement. It requires people to confront uncomfortable truths. Honesty needs us to take responsibility for our actions. By being honest internally, we can cultivate self-development, make meaningful progress and grow personally. Also, honesty contributes to the well-being of the society. Honest people often advocate for fairness and justice. They ensure that information is accurately conveyed and decisions are taken truthfully. This helps to prevent deception and combat unethical practices. In societies where honesty is valued, we witness improved credibility and a good reputation. This creates opportunities, both personally and professionally, as others are more likely to want to collaborate with people who are known for their honesty. Honesty is an essential trait in leadership. Leaders who prioritize honesty inspire trust and motivate others to act with integrity. Living a life with honesty reduces the burden of falsehoods and the need to maintain lies. Honest people experience less stress. They have less inner conflict, as they do not have to constantly build on a pile of lies to avoid being caught.

Additionally, honesty contributes to ethical decision-making. When people prioritize honesty, they consider the impact of their actions. Honest people often uphold moral values, interests of others and follow ethical standards. They are conscious of the consequences of their choices. They strive to act in ways that promote goodness. Honest people also have the courage to speak up against injustice and advocate for positive changes. Their commitment to truth and authenticity inspires others to question unethical practices and work towards creating an inclusive and healthy society.

Honesty is not merely a virtue but a driving force behind ethical decision-making. When we prioritize honesty in our lives, we ignite a chain reaction of empathy, accountability and a shared commitment to create a better world. Let us embrace the transformative power of honesty and become beacons of truth, inspiring those around us to walk the path of integrity, compassion and progress. Together, we can forge a society that thrives on the value of honesty and works hand in hand to build a more just, inclusive and harmonious future for all.

COMPASSION STRENGTHENS BONDS

In the world we live in, tribulations and sufferings are inevitable, making it essential to be compassionate towards each other. Compassion is a moral of being empathetic and concerned about the well-being of others. It is the capacity to understand and share the suffering and joys of others. It is fueled by the desire to eliminate their pain and promote their welfare. Like honesty, compassion shapes our character and has a positive impact on various aspects of our lives and the society. Being compassionate nurtures strong and meaningful relationships. When people are compassionate, they show care and support for each other. Compassionate people actively listen and provide comfort to those in need. By being empathic and kind, we foster an environment of trust, understanding and emotional connection. In compassionate relationships we experience mutual respect, support and have a sense of belonging.

Furthermore, compassion acts as an instrumental in creating inclusive and supportive communities. When we prioritize being compassionate, we actively strive to understand the experiences and needs of others. This moral leads to the promotion of justice and combats discriminatory attitudes and behaviors. Compassionate communities value diversity. They actively work towards creating an environment where all people are valued and empowered. Compassion also plays a huge role in conflict resolution. It promotes peacebuilding. By approaching conflicts with a compassionate mindset, we seek to understand the causes of fights, foster empathy and facilitate reconciliation. Compassionate people find a common ground and work towards mutually benefiting solutions. This leads to the de-escalation of conflicts, promotes peaceful coexistence and contributes to well-being and mental health. When people engage in acts of compassion, such as being kind to others or practicing forgiveness, they experience fulfillment and find purpose. Compassionate behavior stimulates the brain, creating a sense of reward that leads to increased feelings of happiness. Additionally, practicing compassion can reduce stress, promote resilience and enhance overall emotional well-being. Compassion has a life changing impact on societal well-being. Compassionate societies advocate for the welfare and dignity of all members of the community. Compassionate policies and initiatives address disparities, foster inclusivity and prioritize the needs of everyone. Also, compassion inspires acts of service and volunteerism. When people embrace compassion, they often engage in altruistic behaviors and contribute to the welfare of others. Compassionate people responsibly support those who are less fortunate and thus we see interconnectedness. Acts of compassion and service benefit those in need and also cultivate a sense of purpose and meaning to those who extend their hands to help and support others.

Compassion is contagious. When people witness acts of compassion, they are often motivated to emulate similar behaviors. This spreads acts of kindness throughout communities, fostering a culture of caring for each other and social responsibility. People who are compassionate make others feel loved and cared. Compassion is a moral that builds bonds, strengthens relationships and social cohesion. People love the idea of mutual care hence people who are compassionate are often trusted by their families, societies and friends. Having compassion as a moral value enables you to be a reliable person and people will honor you for it.

SHARING FOSTERS COOPERATION

Sharing is a moral value that has been shaping societies since the beginning of human civilization. From the days of hunter-gatherer communities to modern communities, sharing has been ingrained in us as a way to foster cooperation, build trust and ensure the well-being of people and members of our communities. Sharing encompasses the exchange of ideas, knowledge, resources and experiences. It promotes empathy, understanding and interconnectedness among people. In societies that are driven by individualism and self-interest, embodying sharing as a value can have positive impacts. Sharing is an act of generosity and compassion. It reflects a willingness to go beyond our own needs and consider the well-being of others. It is about being selfless. By sharing resources, such as food, shelter or money, we show our concern for the basic needs of others. This act fosters solidarity and community. It builds trust and cooperation among people, creating a supportive network that can withstand adversity. Sharing resources promotes collective progress. Sharing brings people together and cultivates a sense of belonging and connectedness, reminding us that we are all part of a larger community that cares for our well-being. Sharing also extends beyond material possessions. When we share our expertise and teach others, we empower them to grow and develop. Education and knowledge sharing are key drivers of community progress and individual empowerment. By sharing our knowledge, we contribute to the collective wisdom of humanity. This enables others to build upon it and make further advancements. Sharing knowledge also fosters innovation and creativity, as it encourages the exchange of ideas. When we open ourselves up to different views and information, we grow our understanding of the world.

Moreover, sharing has the power to bridge divisions. It fosters understanding among diverse communities. In a globalized world, sharing helps break down barriers of culture, language and geography. When we share our customs, traditions and stories, we invite others into our world. This promotes empathy and respect for different cultures and enables us to recognize our shared humanity. It also helps discover commonalities and recognize that we all face similar joys, challenges and aspirations. By having sharing as a value, we promote inclusivity, equality and social justice, striving for a world where everyone has equal opportunities to thrive. When we share, we experience a sense of purpose and connectedness that transcends material possessions. The act of giving, whether it's a small act of kindness or a larger contribution, has the power to uplift our spirits, strengthen our relationships and foster gratitude for what we have, what we receive and what we give. It reminds us that our happiness is not solely dependent on personal wealth or possessions but is deeply intertwined with the well-being of others. In a world facing numerous challenges, sharing as a value becomes even more critical. Climate change, social inequality and global pandemics are complex problems that require collective action and cooperation. Embracing sharing as a value enables us to address challenges collectively by pooling our resources, knowledge and efforts. Sharing promotes sustainability by encouraging responsible resource use and waste reduction. It also plays a role in addressing social inequalities through the redistribution of resources and opportunities. Sharing allows us to build a society that is more compassionate, resilient and inclusive. The importance of sharing becomes particularly evident in times of crisis. Whether it's a natural disaster, an economic downturn or a global health emergency, sharing plays a crucial role in supporting those affected. In times of crisis, people come together to share resources, provide support and offer comfort. This collective action addresses immediate needs. Sharing in times of crisis strengthens social bonds, restores hope and rebuilds communities. In technology and innovation, sharing has an impact in advancing knowledge and driving progress. Open-source software, for example, relies on the values of collaboration and sharing. Developers from around the world contribute their expertise to create software that is freely available for anyone to use, modify and distribute. This led to remarkable advancements in technology and has fostered a culture of collaboration and innovation. By sharing, we can accelerate progress, solve complex problems and create a more equitable world. In communities when there is inequality and scarcity, the act of sharing can be seen as a threat to personal security or a potential loss of resources. To overcome this mindset we have to recognize that sharing is a way to create abundance and build stronger communities. Sharing involves giving what you have in abundance and receiving what you lack.

RESPECT FOSTERS COEXISTENCE

In most societies, people have different views, religions and cultures, thus respect is vital if we want to coexist with each other and build better communities. Respect involves acknowledging and valuing the dignity and rights of all people. It is the act of treating others well with consideration and fairness, regardless of differences in background and beliefs. Like compassion and honesty, respect also shapes individual character. It fosters healthy relationships. When people have respect for one another, they acknowledge and appreciate each other's unique views and experiences. Respectful people attentively listen, observe, value diversity and engage in meaningful dialogue. By building an environment of mutual respect, we are planting a seed of understanding and coexistence. Respect is essential for building inclusive and cohesive communities. When we value respect, we create an atmosphere where everyone feels acknowledged and accepted.

Respectful communities witness diverse cultures, beliefs and identities. These communities actively work towards eradicating discrimination. By fostering respect for all, communities become more resilient and supportive. Respect enhances effective communication and collaboration. When people treat others with respect, they establish a foundation of openness and honesty. Respectful communication promotes a climate where people feel safe to express themselves, share their ideas and engage in discussions as they know that their opinion is valued.

Moreover, respect contributes to personal well-being and self-esteem. When people are treated with respect, their self-worth and confidence are nurtured. Respectful interactions validate the dignity and value of people and enhance the sense of belonging and self-acceptance. Showing respect for oneself by setting healthy boundaries and practicing self-care promotes overall well-being and positive mental health. Respect has transformative impacts on societal well-being. Respectful societies value fair treatment, regardless of social status, race, gender or any other characteristic. They advocate for human rights to be upheld. Discrimination is challenged and social disparities are addressed. By fostering respect at a societal level, communities can work on building a more just, inclusive and caring society. Respect also inspires positive social change and activism.

When people witness respectful behavior and interactions, it motivates them to work on advocating for justice and the rights of others. Respectful activism leads to the advancement of social causes. Also, respect has a ripple effect, inspiring others to be respectful as well. Like compassion, respect cultivates a sense of inspiration and motivates them to extend the same courtesy and consideration to others. However, this occurs with people who share respect as a moral value.

DISCIPLINE IS ABOUT SELF-CONTROL

One of the most difficult things to do in the modern world is remaining focused and sticking to the plan as the modern world has so much to offer. If you want an ordered life with less frustrations and make progress, discipline is a must-have value. Discipline is all about self-control, self-regulation and following the set values. It is the ability to remain focused and consistent in one's thoughts, actions and behaviors, especially when changes, challenges and temptations arise. When we embody discipline, we cultivate the ability to set goals, create effective strategies and maintain the effort necessary to accomplish the set goals. Disciplined people have self-control, resist distractions and show consistency in their pursuit. Discipline enables us to maximize our potential and achieve success in our endeavors. It also helps build positive habits and overcome tribulations. We establish routines and structures that promote productivity, personal development and well-being by being disciplined. Discipline helps us overcome procrastination, laziness and impulsive behaviors. This then allows us to make progress towards our goals and aspirations. Discipline plays a pivotal role in fostering strong work ethics. When we are disciplined, we show punctuality, reliability and the commitment to work. By being disciplined we prioritize tasks effectively, manage our time efficiently and show accountability in meeting deadlines and fulfilling responsibilities. Disciplined people are valued at work and in communities because they can be relied on to complete jobs and tasks. Moreover, discipline contributes to personal well-being and self-esteem. When people practice discipline, they experience accomplishment and control over their lives. Disciplined people have confidence in their abilities. They engage in healthy behaviors and maintain their lifestyle. They also make choices that promote their well-being. Disciplined people have a more positive impact on the well-being of a society, as they adhere to rules, regulations and duties. They act in accordance with set values and promote order.

Furthermore, discipline in education and institutions fosters a good learning culture. It enables effective teaching and learning. It contributes to the development of responsibility. Through ordered life, disciplined people can inspire and motivate others to adopt discipline. Disciplined people can face challenges and uncertainties. They have the ability to adjust their strategies and learn from failures. Discipline builds a mindset of determination and continuous learning, enabling people and communities to solve problems effectively and with commitment to improve. However it is quite difficult to be disciplined as it requires one to sacrifice and give up on certain things.

Discipline goes hand in hand with being responsible which is all about being accountable for one's actions, choices and obligations. It is about recognizing the impact of one's behavior on oneself, others and the community. Being responsible and being disciplined means you have the courage to take ownership of your actions, decisions and can face consequences that arise from them. Responsible people often show self-discipline, self-control and accountability. They make careful decisions, ensuring that their actions do not cause harm to themselves or anyone else. Prioritizing responsibility as a value helps build a reputation for being dependable, trustworthy and accountable. Both disciplined and responsible people fulfill their commitments, meet deadlines and honor their obligations to others. This reliability fosters trust, as others can rely on them to follow through on their promises and expectations. It is impossible to be disciplined and lack responsibility. Discipline requires responsibility.

Fairness Promotes Trust And Safety

In communities with a variety of cultures, religious interests and a diversity of people, fairness is also a vital value to have. Fairness is the need to treat others impartially and equally. It is the commitment to justice, equality and the absence of favoritism. At its core, fairness establishes a sense of equality in interactions and society. Fair people strive to ensure that everyone is treated with equal respect, consideration and is given the same opportunities. Fair people actively work on eliminating prejudices in their judgments and actions. They create environments where everyone has a fair say and an equal chance to succeed. They also combat discrimination.

Furthermore, fairness promotes trust in relationships. People value fairness, they advocate for the rights of others. Their actions are full of pure intentions and they make others feel valued and respected. In a fair relationship, conflicts are resolved through negotiation, compromise and respect for the rights and perspectives of all parties involved. It is essential to be fair if you want to build inclusive and cohesive communities. When people embrace fairness, they stand against systemic barriers, address social inequalities and promote equal opportunities for all members of society. Fair communities strive to ensure that every person, regardless of their background, is treated with dignity, respect and ensures that they have access to essential resources.

Fairness also creates a sense of belonging, shared values and a collective responsibility towards the well-being of all community members. It also plays a roles in helping people make choices that lead to outcomes that are beneficial to everyone. Fairness creates a room for everyone to communicate their concerns, ideas and perspectives.

When a society values fairness they witness transparency, inclusivity and consideration of diverse perspectives in the governance of their communities. Fair governance ensures that laws, policies and institutions are designed and implemented to promote the well-being and equal treatment of all members of society. Thus creating a community where people are content, secure and have a sense of enjoyment.

Moreover, fairness creates an environment where people can fully participate, thrive and contribute to the progress of society. In addition to personal benefits, fairness promotes social stability, as it addresses grievances, reduces social tensions and fosters a sense of collective responsibility. Safety is one of the key factors people look at when they choose a community to reside in. Fairness and justice are some of the values that enable a community to be safe because when a community values fairness, you know that they are unlikely to cause harm or do anything to make you feel less important.

COURAGE REDEFINES LIMITATIONS

Life is full of surprises, one day everything is well and the other things are not so good. Obstacles arise at any time, even in the journey to pursuing dreams. Thus we need to be courageous. Courage involves the ability to deal with challenges head on and overcome fears. It involves taking risks. It is the act of bravery and standing up for what is right, even when faced with opposition or discomfort. Being courageous pushes people beyond their comfort zones and enables them to face uncertainties. Courageous people pursue their goals and do not fear new beginnings and pioneering. By confronting their fears and ignoring perceived limitations, they open themselves up to growth, self-discovery and life changing experiences. Courage is an essential value. People who possess courage have the ability to challenge injustices, speak out against oppression and voice out new ideas that often improve the way of living. They also take a stand against discrimination, inequality and unethical practices. Their actions inspire others, ignite movements and contribute to positive social transformation. Moreover, courage fosters resilience and perseverance in the face of adversity. Courageous people have resilience and serve as an inspiration to others, showing that we can overcome challenges by facing them, not by running away from them. Courage also helps in making ethical decisions. Courageous people have the strength to make choices based on their own moral values, even when faced with pressure, opposition or temptation to conform. They act with integrity, standing up for what they believe is right and just, even when it may be easier to remain silent or go along with the crowd.

Furthermore, courageous people experience a sense of empowerment, self-assurance and personal fulfillment. Embracing courage helps people break free from self-imposed limitations and live a life aligned with their own values and aspirations. People who are courageous inspire and mobilize others, igniting movements and often changing norms. Their courageous actions inspire collective actions and promote positive social change. Courage builds a society where people are empowered to confront life with confidence and the desire to make changes even when it seems impossible. Courage inspires innovation, progress and breakthroughs. Courageous people explore new possibilities. Their courage to step into the unknown pushes boundaries, redefine limits and pave the way for change.

Humility Cultivates A Balanced Attitude

In the modern era, we find ourselves in a society that rewards self-promotion, individualism and the pursuit of personal success. The rise of social media platforms, where people curate their online personas and showcase their achievements, has further amplified the focus on self-promotion and external validation. In such a society, the value of humility can sometimes be overlooked or misunderstood. However, humility remains a timeless and essential value that holds tremendous value for people and communities alike. It serves as a counterbalance to the self-centeredness and ego-driven mindset. By embracing humility, we can cultivate a more balanced attitude. It also helps ground our perspective and foster growth. Humility is about having a realistic and modest view of oneself. It involves recognizing and accepting one's limitations, weaknesses and imperfections. It is not about self-deprecation or thinking less of oneself, but rather a recognition of the inherent dignity and worth of all people, regardless of their accomplishments or status. It often reminds us that true worth lies beyond external markers of success. It also enables us to appreciate and respect the value of every human being, regardless of their social standing or achievements. Humility encourages us to look beyond ourselves and recognize the contributions and perspectives of others. It is the willingness to learn from others. No matter how knowledgeable and accomplished we may be, there is always more to discover, learn and understand. Humble people approach life with a curiosity and openness, recognizing that they can benefit from the wisdom and experiences of others. They are willing to listen, consider different viewpoints and admit when they don't have all the answers. When people are willing to learn from one another and acknowledge their own fallibility, it becomes easier to work together towards shared goals and find innovative solutions to complex problems.

Moreover, humility allows us to navigate challenges and setbacks with grace and resilience. When we acknowledge our limitations and accept that we are not without shortcomings, it becomes easier to learn from our mistakes and adapt to new circumstances. Humble people seek feedback, reflect on their actions and make necessary adjustments. They are not hindered by the fear of failure. They do not have the need to uphold a perfect image. They instead embrace the growth that comes from accepting imperfections and see their weaknesses as an opportunity to learn more and an invitation for growth. In addition to personal growth, humility plays a significant role in fostering meaningful and fulfilling relationships. Humble people are approachable and down-to-earth. Their friendliness and openness make it easier for others to connect with them.

They listen attentively. They value the perspectives of others, treat everyone with respect and often show kindness for others and themselves. Instead of seeking to assert dominance or prove oneself right, humble people approach disagreements with a willingness to listen, understand and find common ground. This approach promotes constructive dialogue and fosters the building of bridges rather than the creation of divisions. Humility helps to counteract the negative effects of arrogance and entitlement. Arrogance can breed contempt, alienate others and create a toxic atmosphere. In contrast, humility promotes a sense of shared humanity and encourages people to uplift and support one another. It cultivates an environment where people are celebrated for their achievements. In a broader societal context, humility has the power to create a more just and equitable world. By recognizing our own privileges and biases, we become more aware of injustices that exist and are better equipped to dismantle them. Having humility does not mean diminishing aspirations. It is about maintaining a sense of perspective and balance while pursuing personal and professional goals. Humility encourages us to appreciate the contributions of others, acknowledge the role of luck and circumstance in our achievements and use our success to uplift and empower others.

OPTIMISM HELPS MAINTAIN HOPE

Each person faces adversity at one point or another. Adversity and difficulties can not be avoided. To succeed in our endeavors and effectively deal with problems, we need to be optimistic and have a mindset that enables us to see through our obstacles. Optimism is one of the ways to do it. It is about keeping a positive mindset and remaining hopeful in the face of adversity or tribulations. It is the belief that favorable outcomes are possible.

When you are optimistic you believe and hope that obstacles can be overcome. Optimism makes us remain resilient and inspires perseverance. Optimistic people know that challenges are temporary. In difficult situations, they maintain a positive attitude and work towards finding solutions - this enables them to bounce back from setbacks and stay motivated. Optimism helps with maintaining mental health and emotional well-being. When people have an optimistic mindset, they tend to have lower levels of stress and are less anxious about life. Optimistic people focus on embracing the positive aspects of their lives. They notice the good that is going on in their lives and often show gratitude. This positivity increases self-esteem and psychological well-being. Optimism helps us remain calm while we solve problems and make informed decisions.

Furthermore, people who have a positive mindset are likely to explore different perspectives and adapt to changing situations. Their optimism enables them to identify opportunities in unfavorable situations and think clearly under pressure. Being positive radiates enthusiasm and encouragement. Optimistic people uplift others, provide support and inspire those around them. Their positivity fosters strong, meaningful connections and inspires the hope that although things are not expected, they will somehow at one point do. Maintaining a positive mindset enables people to realize their shortcomings and failures as opportunities for growth and learning.

Optimistic people obtain a growth mindset. They believe in their ability to develop new skills and make room for self-improvement. Positivity is one of those values that are contagious if it is practiced well. Being optimistic inspires others to remain hopeful for positive changes and helps envision a better future. It challenges the status quo - how things are. Optimism drives people to take risks, pursue new ideas and contribute to advancements.

Optimistic people inspire creativity. They engage in social initiatives, volunteerism and make efforts to create positive change. They believe in the power of taking action and are motivated to work on things they can control instead of feeling powerless in the face of adversity and difficulties. Their optimism fosters progress.

FORGIVENESS HELPS HEAL WOUNDS

The world we inhabit is full of diverse people, each possessing unique perspectives, cultures, values and characters. In such a dynamic and interconnected world, conflicts and grievances are inevitable. However, forgiveness emerges as a beacon of healing, tolerance and ethical living, offering us a path towards resolution and personal growth. By embracing forgiveness, we can release resentment, let go of past hurts and pave the way for reconciliation.

Forgiveness encompasses more than simply forgetting or overlooking transgressions. It is a profound process that involves healing, understanding and the release of burdensome anger and resentment. When we embark on the journey of forgiveness, we explore its multifaceted nature and recognize its profound impact on our lives, relationships and society as a whole.

At its core, forgiveness is a transformative act that enables us to heal emotional wounds. When we hold onto anger, resentment or a desire for revenge, we allow negative emotions to fester within us, often leading to physical and psychological distress. However, forgiveness provides an opportunity for emotional catharsis, liberating us from the shackles of bitterness and pain. By forgiving, we acknowledge our own humanity and embrace the capacity to let go and move forward.

Moreover, forgiveness is linked to empathy and compassion. To forgive, we must attempt to understand the motivations, circumstances and perspectives of those who have wronged us. This empathetic understanding does not justify or condone their actions, but it grants us the insight to perceive their humanity and acknowledge that their behaviors are often a manifestation of their own struggles and limitations. By extending compassion towards others, we create a space for healing, both for ourselves and for those who have caused us harm.

Forgiveness also plays a crucial role in fostering healthy relationships. In any interpersonal dynamic, conflicts and misunderstandings are inevitable. However, a commitment to forgiveness enables us to navigate these challenges with grace and compassion. By forgiving others, we create an environment of trust, empathy and understanding, laying the foundation for deeper connections and emotional intimacy. Additionally, forgiveness allows us to recognize our own fallibility and seek forgiveness from others, promoting mutual growth and vulnerability.

On a broader scale, forgiveness contributes to societal harmony. In a world where divisions and conflicts persist, the practice of forgiveness becomes even more vital. By forgiving, we break the cycle of vengeance and retribution, fostering an environment of peace, understanding and cooperation. Forgiveness has the power to bridge divides, reconcile communities and promote social healing. It encourages dialogue, empathy and the recognition of our shared humanity, ultimately paving the way for a more compassionate and inclusive society.

Cultivating forgiveness in our lives requires both intention and practice. It begins with acknowledging our own pain and allowing ourselves to grieve. By acknowledging our emotions and seeking support when necessary, we create a space for healing and growth. It is important to note that forgiveness is a personal journey and can take time. It is not a linear process, but rather a series of steps that involve acknowledging the hurt, releasing anger and working towards reconciliation. Forgiveness also involves setting boundaries and taking care of ourselves. While forgiveness is a powerful value, it does not mean tolerating ongoing abuse or harm. It is crucial to prioritize our own well-being and ensure that forgiveness is not mistaken for self-sacrifice or enabling destructive behavior. By establishing healthy boundaries, we protect ourselves while still embracing the transformative power of forgiveness.

GRATITUDE INSPIRES CONTENTMENT

Life is draining. Each day we face different challenges. Some challenges are easy to overcome and others take the best of us. It is important that we keep our heads up and face life with confidence and one way to do just that is by embracing gratitude. Gratitude helps us realize and acknowledge what is going well in our lives. Gratitude is the practice that involves cultivating a mindset of appreciation for the present moment. It is about recognizing the abundance that exists within and around us, even in the face of bad times. When we are grateful, we are able to shift our perspective, enabling us to see positivity and abundance. When we focus on what we already have instead of what we lack, we become aware of the blessings that surround us. Gratitude enables us to realize the simple pleasures, the relationships that nourish us and the opportunities that come our way. Directing our attention to these aspects, cultivates fulfillment regardless of the circumstances we find ourselves in.

One of the impacts of practicing gratitude is the influence it has on mental health. Gratitude reduces stress and depression. By expressing gratitude we allow our brains to make changes, changes that weaken negative emotions and strengthen positive emotions. This fosters a sense of self-awareness. This awareness then enables us to savor life's experiences and fully engage in present moments.

Rather than thinking about our past, being regretful and anxious about the future, gratitude keeps us engaged in what's going on in the moment. It enables us to make the most of every moment.

Furthermore, when we express gratitude to others, we strengthen our bonds with them. By appreciating and acknowledging the kindness and support we receive from others, we foster a culture of giving and receiving. Gratitude has the power to grow our ability to be empathetic and compassionate. As we are aware of the blessings in our own lives, we develop care and we are able to understand and share struggles and challenges faced by others. This empathy drives us to work on improving the well-being of people around us. Gratitude inspires us to offer support. The practice of gratitude is not limited to personal benefits; it can also be found in workplaces. Workplaces that promote gratitude increase employee satisfaction and productivity. When employees are appreciated, they are likely to come to work constantly and work passionately. Gratitude in the workplace strengthens teamwork. It promotes collaboration and creates a good work environment that encourages innovation, creativity and overall organizational success.

Developing Moral Values

Moral values shape our character. Basically our moral values define who we are because they influence our decisions and how we interact with others. This makes it crucial to develop and nurture moral values. In this chapter I hope to provide a short rather insightful guidance on how to cultivate moral values and emphasize the fact that growth is an ongoing process.

One of the ways to develop moral values is by recognizing the impact of moral values and doing some self-reflection and introspection. This process involves taking the time to identify and clarify one's personal ethics and reflect on the values that matter most. By asking ourselves important questions, such as "What kind of person do I aspire to be?" and "What kind of life do I want to live?", we can gain clarity about ourselves and the kind of person we aim to become. Self-reflection is about exploring our inner beliefs and enabling us to make conscious choices. It is a process of introspection that encourages us to examine our actions and thoughts. By understanding the motivation behind our behaviors, we can then come to realize how our actions impact others and the world around us.

During self-reflection, it is important to think about what brings us peace, fulfillment and what aspects of life truly matter to us? By identifying these values, we can then prioritize them when making decisions and ensure that our actions align with our aspirations. For instance, if we value honesty and integrity, we have to look at whether we uphold these in our lives. Once we have clarity about ourselves and the kind of life we wish to live, the next step is to align our actions and choices with the values we have identified as mattering the most for us. Through examining each situation and considering how our choices align with our moral values, we can act in a way that slowly builds us to be the desired self.

Aligning our actions with our moral values often involves making difficult choices and sacrifices. It may require us to prioritize long-term benefits over short-term gains or to challenge norms that contradict our values. For example, if you value family then you must give up or limit going out with your peers more often and instead spend more time with your family. Staying true to our values cultivates a good character and often makes us role models to those who aspire for the same life we live. As a result, we inspire them to live by their own values as well. Developing good morals also involves recognizing our imperfections and being open to changes. As we engage in self-reflection, we discover our shortcomings. This discovery should not discourage us;

instead it should motivate us to acknowledge where we fall short and strive for improvement. By acknowledging our flaws and working on them, we show humility and a commitment to better ourselves.

Another effective way to develop and nurture moral values is by seeking inspiration from moral role models. While self-reflection and introspection are vital, looking up to people who embody the values we admire can provide additional guidance and motivation on our moral journey. Moral role models can come from various spheres of life, including leaders, family members, celebrities or even fictional characters. These people often have the qualities and live the kind of lifestyle that resonates with our aspirations. By studying their lives, actions and the values they uphold, we can gain valuable insights and inspiration for integrating those values into our own lives. Family members, especially those who have shown strong moral character can also be influential role models. By observing how they deal with challenges and make decisions based on their values, we can learn more about moral integrity. Despite their public personas, celebrities can also serve as moral role models. Some people in the public eye advocate for important causes and have values that align with our own. By studying how their moves, their endeavors and dedication to growth, we can find inspiration to engage in similar efforts. Although they are not so real, fictional characters as well can still provide us with insights about moral values. Characters can sometimes represent ideals we strive to embody. By examining their journeys and the choices they make, we can learn about the importance of bravery, compassion, integrity and other values.

Observing and learning from moral role models enables us to see how values can be put into practice. By studying the actions of our moral role models, we can gain practical knowledge about how to integrate these values into our daily lives. This involves understanding the underlying values that guide their behavior. Incorporating the values of our moral role models into our own lives involves constantly aligning our actions with the values we admire. By drawing inspiration from moral role models, we can develop a strong moral compass and enable ourselves to live a life guided by our values. While looking up to our moral role models, it is important to note that no person is perfect. Blindly following someone without considering the potential flaws in their behavior can lead to misguided choices. For us to avoid being misguided, we have to evaluate the values and actions of our role models, taking what resonates with us and leaving behind what does not.

Moral values should not remain concepts; they need to be practiced in our daily lives. One effective way to accomplish this is by setting goals and taking actions that are aligned with our values. By doing so, we can establish a clear intention and commitment to living according to our moral values. For instance, if honesty is one of our values, we can make a conscious decision to always speak the truth, even when it becomes inconvenient to do so. This commitment to truthfulness establishes a foundation for integrity in our interactions. It requires us to be mindful of our words and actions, ensuring that they consistently reflect our commitment to honesty. If we practice this enough eventually it becomes a habit, something we do unconsciously - without even thinking about it. It is crucial to seek opportunities to live by our values. This means engaging in situations where our moral values can be put into practice. Also, we have to regularly evaluate our actions and choices to ensure that they align with our moral compass. We should regularly reflect upon and assess how our behaviors and decisions align with our values. This enables us to identify areas that need improvement. It provides an opportunity for growth and refinement of our character. When we evaluate our actions, it is important to be honest and objective. We should critically analyze whether our behaviors align with our stated values and the impact our behaviors have. This is so that we learn from our mistakes. Integrating moral values into our daily lives requires consistency. It is not always easy. It requires us to make difficult choices and face uncomfortable situations. However, the benefits of living in accordance with our values outweigh the challenges. When our actions align with our values, we live a life of integrity, fulfillment and inner peace as a result.

Developing and nurturing moral values is a lifelong journey that requires conscious effort and commitment. By understanding the importance of moral values, reflecting on personal ethics, seeking inspiration from moral role models and actually practicing actions that align with our values, we can lay a solid foundation for our moral growth. This allows us to cultivate a strong sense of integrity and make ethical choices that positively impact ourselves and those around us.

One key aspect of developing moral values is understanding their significance. Recognizing the profound impact our values have on our decisions and relationships enables us to approach them with intention and mindfulness. This self-awareness prompts us to reflect on our personal ethics, assessing the values and beliefs that guide our behavior. It encourages us to question and refine our values, ensuring they align with our authentic selves. Also, seeking inspiration from moral role models can help shape our ethical compass. Observing people who embody the values we aspire to cultivate provides us with guidance and motivation. Whether it is a historical figure, a family member, or a community leader, their actions can serve as a moral compass and encourage us to strive for similar values. However, merely understanding and seeking inspiration is not enough. We must actively practice actions that align with our values. This involves making conscious choices that reflect our moral values in our daily lives. It means treating others with respect, practicing empathy and compassion and promoting fairness and justice.

By actively incorporating these strategies and exercises into our lives, we can experience personal growth and fulfillment. Our moral development becomes a transformative journey that shapes our character and enriches our lives. Through continuous self-reflection, conscious choices and the influence of positive role models, we can navigate the complexities of ethical dilemmas and build a strong moral foundation that guides us towards a more virtuous and meaningful existence.

EMBRACE YOUR MORAL VALUES

While or after you have done some self-reflection and practiced your moral values, be aware that not everyone around you will share the same values and dreams. As you strive to build a character rooted in honesty, compassion, sharing, respect, discipline, fairness, courage, humility, optimism, forgiveness, gratitude and self-reflection, you may encounter criticism and resistance from those who do not align with your values or aspirations.

It is not uncommon for people who do not share your moral values to criticize or question your choices. Some may view your commitment to honesty as overly blunt or insensitive, failing to understand the importance of truthfulness in your interactions. Others might perceive your compassionate nature as a sign of weakness, not comprehending the power and strength that empathy and understanding can bring to your relationships.

Similarly, your dedication to sharing and giving may be misinterpreted as naivety or a lack of self-preservation. Those who prioritize their self-interests above all else may struggle to grasp the value of generosity and selflessness in building a more equitable and harmonious society.

Your unwavering respect for others, regardless of their background or beliefs, might be met with resistance from people who hold prejudiced views or engage in discriminatory behavior. Challenging the status quo and advocating for fairness and equality can be met with opposition from those who benefit from the existing systems of privilege and power.

Moreover, as you strive to embody courage in standing up for what is right and challenging injustices, you may face backlash from those who prefer to maintain the status quo or avoid confronting uncomfortable truths. The courage to initiate change and promote positive transformation can be unsettling for those who fear disruption or losing their positions of authority.

Embracing humility and acknowledging your limitations and imperfections may be seen as a lack of self-confidence or a sign of weakness by people who prioritize self-aggrandizement and arrogance. The value of humility in building authentic and meaningful connections with others might be undervalued or misunderstood.

Furthermore, maintaining an optimistic outlook and believing in the potential for positive change might be perceived as unrealistic or overly idealistic by people who dwell in pessimism and negativity. Your commitment to hope and resilience in the face of challenges may challenge the worldview of those who see obstacles as insurmountable barriers.

While your practice of forgiveness can promote healing and reconciliation, some might misunderstand your willingness to forgive as a sign of passivity or an invitation for further harm. Advocating for accountability and personal growth alongside forgiveness may be necessary to ensure that your boundaries are respected.

In expressing gratitude for the blessings and experiences in your life, you may encounter skepticism or envy from people who struggle to find contentment or are envious of your achievements. Recognizing and addressing negative emotions in a healthy way is essential to maintain emotional well-being while practicing gratitude.

Engaging in self-reflection and striving for personal growth might be met with resistance from those who prefer to remain stagnant or avoid facing their own shortcomings. Some may perceive self-reflection as unnecessary or uncomfortable, failing to recognize its role in fostering self-awareness and continuous improvement.

In the face of criticism and resistance, it is essential to stand your ground and do justice to yourself by remaining steadfast in your commitment to your moral values and aspirations. While it can be tempting to change your goals or alter your behavior to please others, compromising your integrity and authenticity would be a disservice to yourself and the values you hold dear.

Instead, embrace your moral values as guiding principles that shape your character and actions. Be confident in the positive impact these values have on your life and the lives of those around you. Remember that living in alignment with your moral compass contributes to a more compassionate, just and harmonious world.

When faced with criticism, approach it with an open mind and a willingness to listen to different perspectives. While you may not be able to change the opinions of others, understanding their viewpoints can help you strengthen your arguments and refine your understanding of your values.

Stay true to your convictions and when necessary, advocate for the importance of these moral values in fostering personal growth and building a better society. Lead by example, demonstrating through your actions how living in accordance with these values can promote positive change and enrich your life and the lives of others.

Surround yourself with people who share your moral values and support your aspirations. Building a supportive community of like-minded people can provide encouragement, validation and strength during challenging times.

Lastly, remember that personal growth and character-building are ongoing journeys. Embrace the process of continuous improvement and self-discovery, recognizing that challenges and criticism are opportunities for growth and refinement.

As you engage in self-reflection and practice your moral values, be prepared to encounter criticism and resistance from those who do not share the same values and dreams. Standing your ground and remaining true to your convictions is crucial in building a character grounded in integrity, compassion and purpose. Embrace the positive impact of these moral values on your life and the lives of others and advocate for their importance in shaping a more compassionate and harmonious world. By staying committed to your values, surrounding yourself with supportive people and continuously seeking personal growth, you can confidently navigate the complexities of life while building a character that reflects your most cherished values and aspirations.

BALANCING MORAL VALUES

Although moral values such as honesty, compassion, sharing, respect, discipline, fairness, courage, humility, optimism, forgiveness, gratitude and self-reflection have a positive impact in our lives, fostering trust, empathy and personal growth, it is worth noting that blindly over-practicing these values can lead to certain negativities. While they form the foundation of a compassionate and harmonious society, it is important to be aware of the potential challenges that arise when these values are taken to extremes without thoughtful consideration.

Honesty, when practiced without tact and sensitivity, can become hurtful and damaging to relationships. While being truthful is commendable, being overly blunt or straightforward can ignore the emotional impact of our words on others. It is important to balance honesty with compassion, choosing our words carefully and delivering truth with empathy.

Excessive compassion can lead to enabling behavior, where people become overly nurturing and rescuing, preventing others from taking responsibility for their own growth and development. It is essential to establish healthy boundaries and encourage people to find their own solutions while offering support and guidance.

Indiscriminate sharing, while promoting a sense of community, can leave us vulnerable to exploitation. Some people may take advantage of our willingness to share resources, time, or money, leading to burnout or financial strain. It is important to evaluate the intentions of those seeking assistance and ensure our generosity is balanced and sustainable.

Overemphasizing respect for others can result in neglecting self-respect. This can lead to allowing others to mistreat us or compromising our own well-being for the sake of maintaining harmony. It is crucial to recognize that respect is a two-way street and to treat ourselves with the same dignity and consideration we give to others.

Excessive discipline can manifest as perfectionism and self-criticism, hindering our ability to embrace imperfections and learn from mistakes. It is important to practice self-compassion, acknowledging that mistakes are a natural part of growth and to set realistic standards for ourselves.

An obsession with fairness can lead to a rigid adherence to values, disregarding the unique circumstances and needs of people. This can unintentionally cause harm and prevent us from considering alternative perspectives. It is essential to balance fairness with empathy, taking into account the context of each situation and the individual needs of those involved.

Over-practicing courage can result in unnecessary confrontations that alienate others and hinder constructive dialogue. It is important to choose our battles wisely, approaching conflicts with an open mind and a willingness to listen.

Being overly humble can lead to self-effacement, where we downplay our strengths and contributions, hindering personal growth and recognition. It is crucial to acknowledge our own worth and embrace self-confidence while remaining open to learning from others.

Blind optimism can blind us to potential risks and challenges, leaving us unprepared for adversity. It is important to balance positivity with realism, maintaining a hopeful outlook while also being aware of potential obstacles and preparing for them.

Frequent forgiveness without accountability can perpetuate toxic relationships and enable harmful behavior without consequences. It is important to set boundaries and recognize when forgiveness should be accompanied by accountability to promote healthy relationships and personal well-being.

Excessive gratitude can suppress genuine emotions and legitimate grievances, resulting in a lack of assertiveness and emotional suppression. It is crucial to practice gratitude while also acknowledging and addressing negative emotions in a healthy way.

Intensive self-reflection can lead to self-doubt and rumination, inhibiting progress and decision-making. It is important to use self-reflection as a tool for growth rather than self-criticism, practicing self-compassion and focusing on learning and improvement.

To avoid the negativities that may arise from over-practicing these values, it is crucial to adopt a balanced and discerning approach. Practicing these values with thoughtfulness and self-awareness allows us to harness their transformative power while avoiding the potential pitfalls. We can avoid the negativity associated with these values by being mindful of our words and considering their impact on others when practicing honesty. Setting healthy boundaries and encouraging self-responsibility helps prevent enabling behavior. Evaluating intentions and maintaining a balance in sharing ensures our generosity is sustainable. Balancing respect for others with self-respect promotes healthy relationships. Embracing self-compassion and setting realistic standards prevents the negative effects of excessive discipline. Combining fairness with empathy allows for a more nuanced understanding of individual circumstances. Choosing battles wisely and approaching conflicts with openness and willingness to listen fosters constructive dialogue. Acknowledging our strengths and contributions while remaining open to learning promotes a healthy balance of humility. Balancing optimism with realism helps us prepare for challenges while maintaining a positive outlook. Combining forgiveness with accountability ensures personal growth and healthy relationships. Practicing gratitude while also addressing negative emotions allows for emotional well-being. Using self-reflection as a tool for growth and improvement rather than self-criticism promotes progress and decision-making.

Moral values have a positive impact on our lives, shaping our relationships and personal growth. However, blindly over-practicing these values can lead to negativities. By adopting a balanced and discerning approach, we can navigate these challenges and harness the transformative power of these values. Practicing these values with thoughtfulness, self-awareness and consideration of the broader context allows us to experience their benefits while avoiding the potential pitfalls. By finding a harmonious balance in our actions and interactions, we can contribute to a more compassionate and harmonious world.

Epilogue

As we come to the end of our journey through "The Art of Morality: Understanding Moral Values," it becomes evident that morality is not merely an abstract concept but a guiding force that shapes our lives and relationships. This book has explored various moral values, highlighting their significance and impact on our personal growth and the well-being of our communities. By reflecting on these teachings, we find ourselves equipped with valuable insights that can shape our actions and contribute to a more compassionate and harmonious world.

The initial chapters laid a strong foundation, providing us with a comprehensive understanding of morals and their profound influence in our lives. They reminded us that morality is not a set of rigid rules but a flexible framework that adapts to the complexities of human existence. By delving into the essence of moral values, we discovered their ability to guide our decisions, choices and interactions, ultimately shaping our character and impacting the world around us.

Throughout the book, we explored a range of moral values, each carrying its unique significance. We learned about the power of honesty, which builds trust and fosters genuine connections in our relationships. Honesty demands courage and self-reflection, as it requires us to confront our own truths and communicate them with integrity.

Compassion emerged as a crucial value, teaching us to cultivate empathy and understanding towards others. Compassion serves as a bridge that connects people, transcending differences and fostering a sense of unity. By embodying compassion, we alleviate suffering, extend a helping hand and create a world that embraces the inherent value of every human being.

The value of sharing was emphasized, highlighting generosity and selflessness as fundamental elements of creating a more equitable society. Sharing fosters a sense of community, promoting cooperation and solidarity among people. By recognizing and sharing our resources, knowledge and experiences, we create a ripple effect of positive change, uplifting not only ourselves but also those around us.

Respect, too, played a crucial role, reminding us of the importance of treating others with dignity and recognizing their inherent worth. Respect fosters harmonious relationships, cultivates tolerance and encourages open-mindedness. By practicing respect, we create an environment that celebrates diversity and promotes inclusivity, allowing for the flourishing of individual and collective potential.

Discipline emerged as a value that instills self-control, perseverance and the ability to make intentional choices aligned with our values. By embracing discipline, we empower ourselves to overcome challenges, resist temptations and nurture our moral compass in the face of adversity.

Fairness was explored as an essential value, compelling us to consider the perspectives of others, advocate for equality and challenge systems of oppression. By striving for fairness, we contribute to the creation of a just society where everyone has an equal opportunity to thrive.

Courage was highlighted as a key value, enabling us to stand up for what is right and face our fears. Courage allows for ethical action, even in the face of adversity and opposition. By summoning our courage, we can effect positive change, challenge injustices and inspire others to do the same.

Humility emerged as a powerful value, teaching us the importance of recognizing our limitations, learning from others and embracing a mindset of continuous growth.

Humility creates a foundation for genuine connection, empathy and self-improvement.

Optimism was explored as a transformative mindset that allows us to see the potential for positive change, inspiring hope and resilience. By nurturing an optimistic outlook, we become catalysts for progress and inspire others to persevere in the pursuit of moral ideals.

The significance of forgiveness was recognized, as it has the power to heal wounds and foster reconciliation. Forgiveness liberates us from the burden of resentment and allows for personal growth, understanding and the restoration of relationships. By embracing forgiveness, we break the cycle of negativity and create opportunities for healing and renewal.

Gratitude was emphasized as a value that cultivates appreciation for the blessings and experiences in our lives. Gratitude encourages mindfulness, humility and a sense of interconnectedness. By practicing gratitude, we cultivate a positive mindset, deepen our relationships and recognize the abundance present in our lives.

Finally, self-reflection and aligning our actions with our moral values were discussed, highlighting the importance of evaluating our choices, behaviors and intentions. Through self-reflection and introspection, we continually refine our understanding of morality and strive to live authentically and ethically.

As we conclude our exploration of moral values, it is important to remember that this journey is ongoing. "The Art of Morality: Understanding Moral Values" serves as a guide, inspiring us to cultivate the highest ideals within ourselves and embrace the transformative power of moral values in shaping a more just, compassionate and harmonious world.

May the lessons from this book inspire us to embody honesty, compassion, sharing, respect, discipline, fairness, courage, humility, optimism, forgiveness, gratitude and self-reflection as we navigate the intricate tapestry of life. By doing so, we become agents of positive change, influencing not only our own well-being but also the collective destiny of humanity.